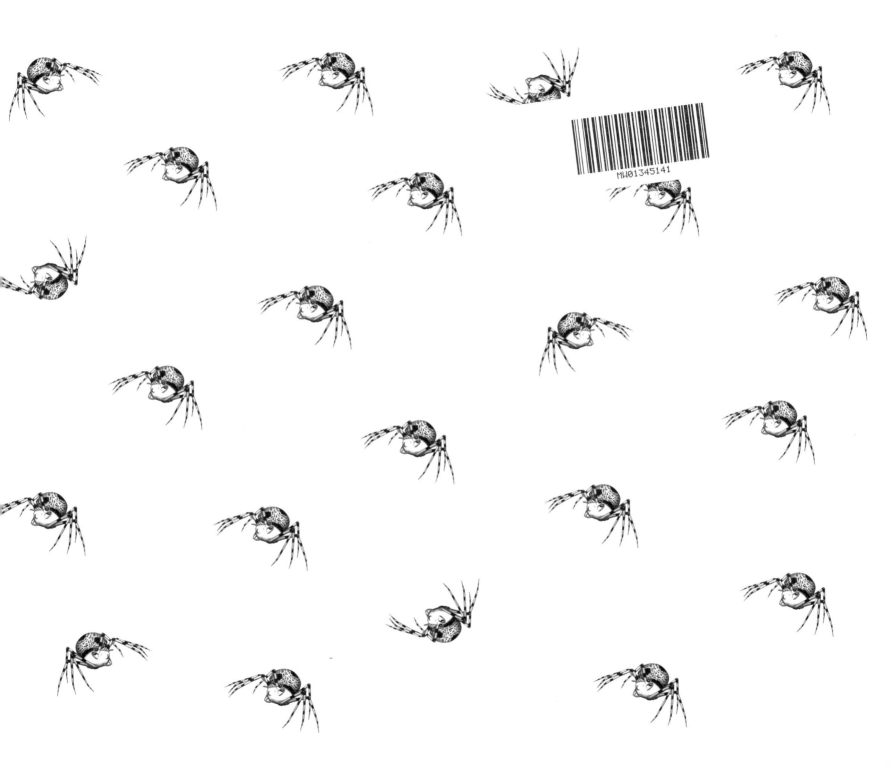

THE RAINBOW WEB

written by Cheryl Block

illustrated by Gene Takeshita

©2005 BLOCK PUBLISHING
www.blockpub.com
All rights reserved
ISBN 0-9761625-0-4
Printed in China

I dedicate this book and CD to
the two people who helped bring it to life,
my illustrator, Gene Takeshita, and
my multimedia designer, Jeffrey Reynolds.
Thank you both so much.

Cheryl Block is an educator and writer. She has multiple teaching credentials, including a Master's in special education and twelve years' experience as a special educator. She has worked in educational publishing for the last ten years and has authored three books of her own, as well as collaborating on numerous others. Her daughter is a kindergarten teacher and her son is in college.

Gene Takeshita is a freelance designer and illustrator. His work has included history and science museum exhibitions, an aquarium, graphic design, art direction, poster, editorial, and biological illustration. One of his areas of special interest is storytelling and illustrating the natural world. He lives with his wife in Monterey, CA, and they have one daughter.

Jeffrey Reynolds has extensive knowledge of both science and technology. He specializes in the design and production of educational materials using interactive computer technologies. He has created multimedia exhibits, web sites, and CD-Roms for clients that include the Monterey Bay Aquarium, Disney, and Apple Computer. Jeff's goal is to make science fun!

The little spider loved the beautiful web he spun each day.

It was almost invisible, except when the sunlight shone through the transparent threads.

But the little spider especially loved the drops of morning dew that covered the silken threads with tiny rainbows.

Wouldn't it be wonderful to have a web of many colors, he thought.

One day, a bird flying overhead dropped a bit of red berry from its beak. A drop of red juice splashed onto the little spider's web.

The little spider hurried to the red drop and took a sip. Delicious!

As the little spider began to spin his web the next morning, he saw that the fine threads were colored red. How wonderful!

The other spiders came to admire his work. They'd never seen anything like it.

Perhaps, thought the little spider, the same thing might happen if he tried some other berries.

He looked about him. A blueberry bush grew not far away.

The little spider crawled to the bush and found some crushed berries on the ground. He sipped the juice. Not bad!

The next morning, there were blue threads woven among the red ones. The little spider was so excited!

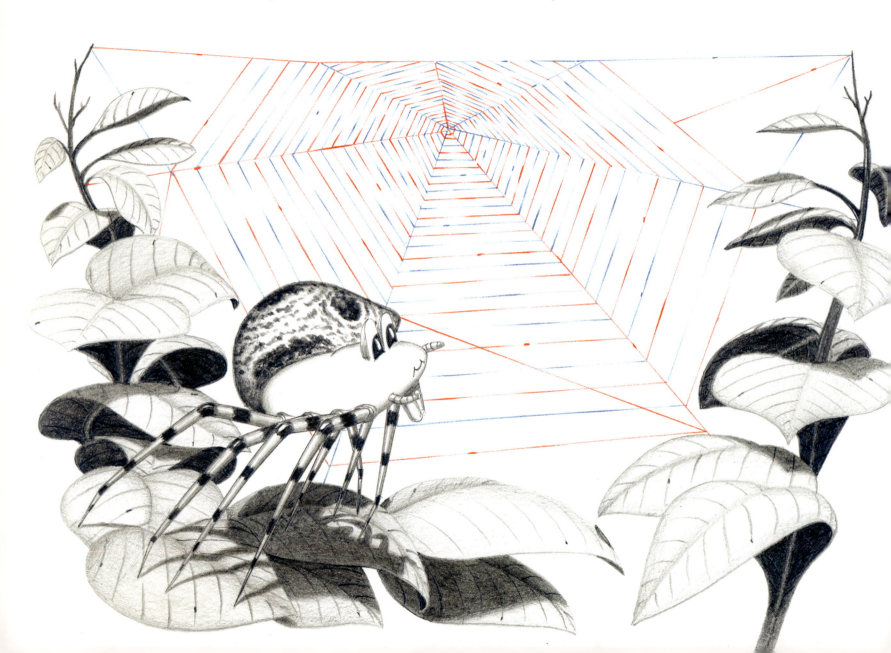

Each night, he went looking for a different colored berry.
And each morning he added a new color to his web.

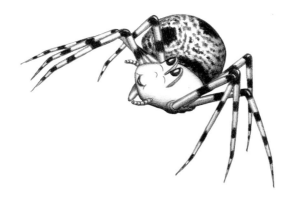

He found dark purple blackberries.

He found golden yellow berries and shiny orange berries.

He found bright green berries.

Soon he had made a web of all the colors.
A rainbow web!

All the other spiders admired his web. The little spider was so proud.

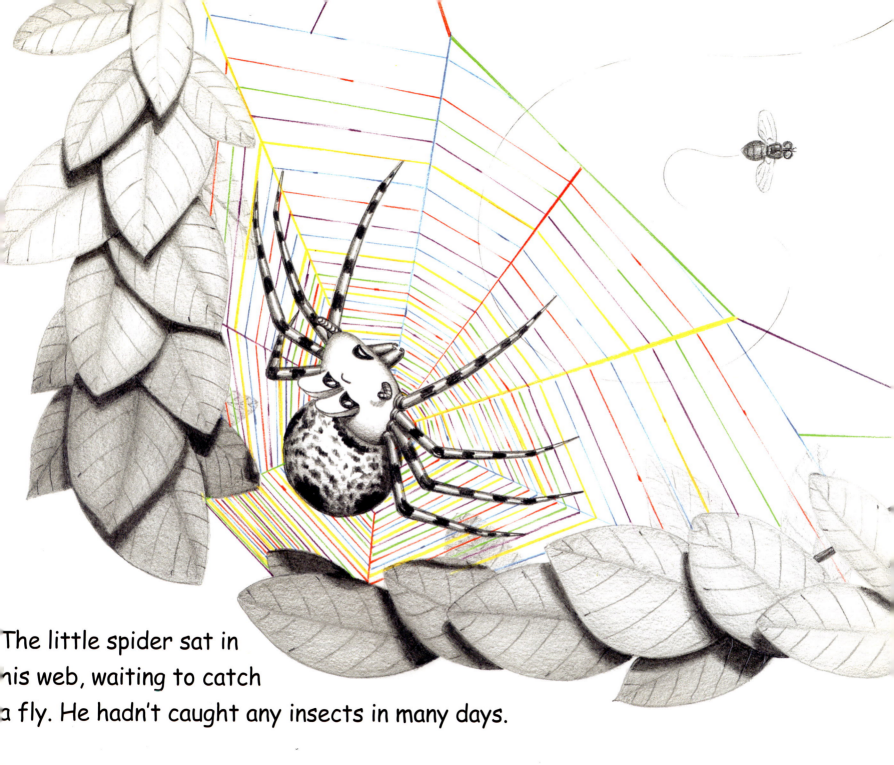

The little spider sat in his web, waiting to catch a fly. He hadn't caught any insects in many days.

As a matter of fact, the flies hadn't even come near his web.

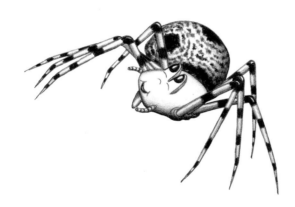

He realized he was very, very hungry. A day went by and then another. Still no flies landed in the little spider's web.

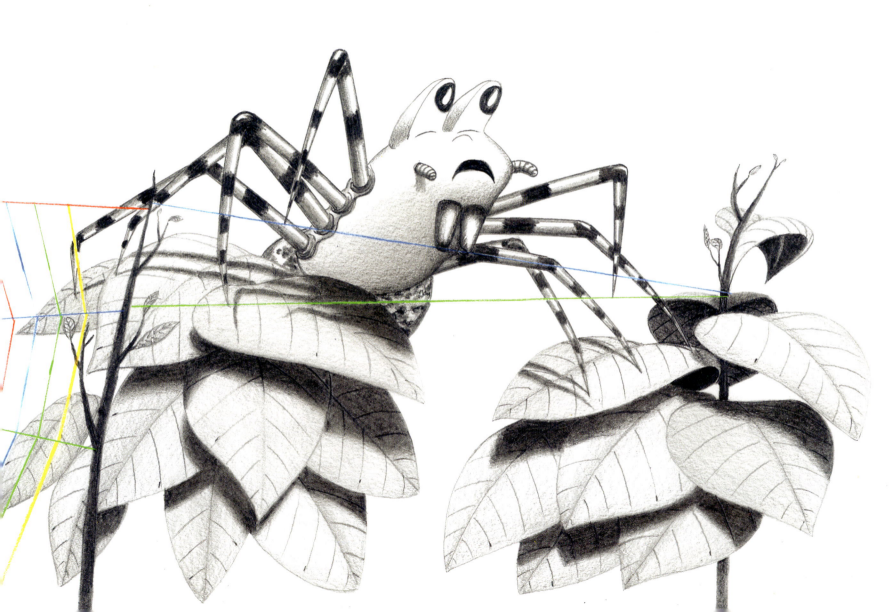

He decided to go to his father and ask him what was wrong.

"Father, I have made a beautiful rainbow web that all the other spiders admire."

"That is true, my little spider."

"But the insects don't land in my web anymore, Father. I am so hungry. Why can't I catch any flies?"

"Beautiful as your rainbow web may be, there's a reason why spiders' webs are almost invisible. We do not have wings like the flies and gnats, so we cannot chase after them.

"We are like fishermen with their nets.
We catch food with our webs.

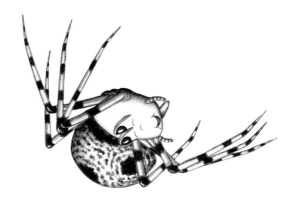

"The flies can now see your colorful web, and they stay away from it. That is why you have not caught any food."

The next morning, the little spider spun a transparent web and quickly caught a juicy fly for breakfast.

All was now right with the world, thought the little spider, as he admired the tiny rainbow in a corner of his web.

The Rainbow Web book and CD offer parents, teachers, and homeschoolers a complete thematic unit on spiders that meets state and national standards for both science and literature, as well as offering cross-curricular activities in math and reading

The enclosed CD teaches the science behind the story. It includes units on spider and insect anatomy, types of spiders and spider webs, primary and secondary colors, and rainbows. Each unit has a narrated lesson with interactive activities to reinforce the information taught. There is a narrated copy of the story that the child can listen to independently. Also included are reproducible activity sheets in math, reading, and science that parents and teachers can print to accompany the CD lessons.

The CD requires no installation and works on both Windows and Macintosh. The software is easy and fun for young children to use. Children have the option of reading the material or having it read to them. Single copies of the CD are available for purchase, as well as multi-user licenses for classrooms and labs. CD requirements are listed below:

Be sure to visit our website: www.blockpub.com. for more activities to go with our books and software.

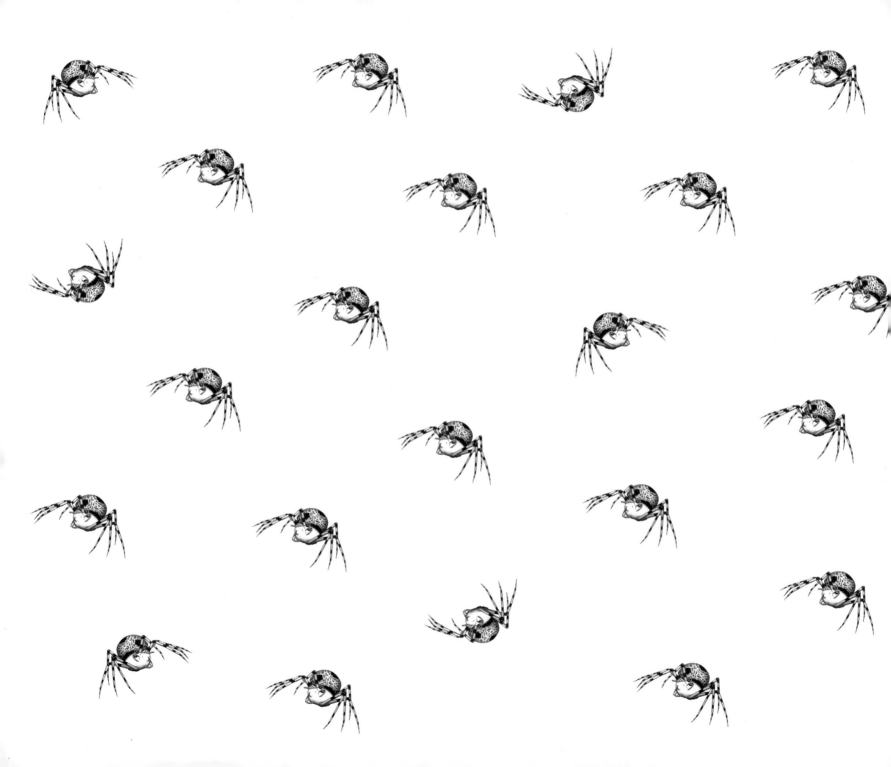